Walter Pfeiffer

text adapted from an original by Marianne Héron

LIVING IN
IRELAND

Flammarion

Paris - New York

CONTENTS

FOREWORD

Getting to know any country is a process of discovery which invariably involves filtering a kaleidoscope of visual impressions, sifting the clues they contain to the understanding of the nation and its people.

For many years, I have studied and photographed Ireland's rich and colorful landscapes. Inspired by the wish to penetrate the secrets of its remotest corners, I have given way on numerous occasions to the temptation to follow twisting paths or ignore "No trespassing" signs, with the result that some breathtaking images are now indelibly imprinted on my memory. I can see now the silvery light reflected in the windows of a castle whose walls loomed above me in the twilight chill. I shall always remember the soft blue limewashed walls of a welcoming cottage, firmly

Irish landscapes: from County Donegal in the north (pp. 1 and 4–5) to County Wexford in the south (pp. 2–3), by way of Connemara (p. 6 and opposite), the Aran Islands (pp. 8 and 9) and the national park of Glenveigh in County Donegal (below).

planted on the coastline overlooking an ever-changing sea. Nor shall I easily forget the warmth and hospitality offered by a doorway opening to reveal a hallway paved with worn flags. In searching out and photographing—with equal delight—both immense panoramas and unexpected architectural details from a whole range of periods and styles, I found I had embarked on a quest for the very spirit of Ireland, and I have tried to share my love for this wonderful country, its originality, its diversity, and its riches. I hope that the images in this book may open doors for you into warm rooms in rich tones of ocher and burgundy, lit by the golden light of a peat fire and with the green of the Irish countryside filtering gently through their windows.

WALTER PFEIFFER

IRISH TOWNS

The geographical positions, names, and street plans of Irish towns provide a tremendous number of clues to their history. Ireland was originally a country of herdsmen, with no tradition of urban life: indeed, the only centers of any importance were the great monasteries of Ireland's golden age, of the time of saints and clerics. In the ninth century, Viking invaders founded settlements on the southeast coast, as well as at Dublin, Limerick, and Waterford, but it was not until after the arrival of the Normans, in 1169, that villages began to grow up in the interior of the country.

Only during the relative peace of the eighteenth century did the urban fabric of Ireland really start to develop. The great expansion of provincial towns dates from the early nineteenth century, before the Great Famine caused by the potato blight, with its disastrous consequences for both the population and the economy.

The heart of Dublin, divided by the dark waters of the Liffey (opposite). Dublin's pubs (above) are an essential part of life in the city.
Overleaf: The magnificent eighteenth-century Four Courts, where the public may attend sittings.

A desire for peace and harmony was a significant influence on the layout of many of Ireland's provincial towns, architecture being viewed as a means of expressing the strength of their unity and corporate spirit. Main streets were widened and imposing public buildings sprang up: courthouses, town halls, and market halls, all conceived as meeting places for the local community.

The most celebrated example of urban development in Ireland is to be found without doubt in the streets and squares of Georgian Dublin. In the eighteenth century, Dublin was frequently described as the "second city of Europe," and as seat of the Irish parliament and of the viceroy's official residence, it was a center of considerable importance. Influential families bought or rented elegant mansions in the city, close to the centers of power, in order to promote their interests more effectively. It was during the second half of the eighteenth century, known as the Irish Renaissance, that the Georgian heart of Dublin was built.

These Georgian town residences were intended to impress visitors to the city. While the style of their facades remained largely unaltered in the century between 1730 and 1830, their interior decoration was modified over the years to suit changing fashions. In stucco work, for example, coffered ceilings—designed to conceal the beams—disappeared in about 1740, to be replaced by elaborate decors in the baroque or rococo style. Introduced to Ireland by the Francini brothers, Italian stucco-workers of great repute, the baroque was subsequently taken up by Irish craftsmen, including the celebrated Robert West. After 1760, the influence of the Scottish architects Robert and James Adam ushered in the vogue for motifs in the neoclassical manner, a style adopted with most success by the Irish decorative artist Michael Stapleton.

Many of the streets and squares of central Dublin owe their generous proportions to the Wide Streets Commission, set up in 1757. Curiously, rather than being governed by any overall plan, the houses that lined these new boulevards sprang up piecemeal, with landowners building two or three houses on each plot of land, generally

This attractive horse-drawn barouche for delivering whiskey can still be seen in the streets of Dublin today (above). The facades of the houses in a small town in County Cork (opposite), painted in pastel colors in typically Irish fashion, bear witness to the individualism of the national character.

keeping one for their own use and renting out the others.

Very few of these houses remain as private dwellings today, the great majority having been carved up and converted into hotels, offices, or apartments. But a few courageous architectural enthusiasts have set out to restore some of them to their former glory, thus saving part of the nation's heritage which was in danger of being lost forever.

With the Act of Union of 1801, the Irish parliament ceased to exist and Dublin's age of expansion drew to a close. Thereafter famine and economic decline combined to put a stop to urban growth in general until the reigns of Queen Victoria and Edward VII. The successive layers of these architectural era are as clearly visible in the fabric of Irish towns as the rings on a venerable tree stump.

Nowadays, the villas and mansions erected in the Victorian period to accommodate the expanding middle classes are once more highly prized, enjoying—like former craft workshops—a new prestige.

The cycle thus turns full circle, as in James Joyce's description of Dublin in *Ulysses*: "Cityful passing away, another cityful coming, passing away too: another coming on, passing on."

This elegant house in a part of the city to the south of the Liffey boasts one of Dublin's most exquisite Georgian door surrounds. A stroll through Merrion Square—one of the loveliest squares in the city and a superb example of Georgian town-planning which has survived virtually intact—reveals the full charm of these graceful houses.

The drawing room in shades of pale gold makes a handsome setting for a fine collection of Chinese vases, some of which are displayed on a giltwood console table from Limerick. This house, lovingly restored by its owner, is open to visitors by appointment.

This eighteenth-century house, now gradually being restored, is to be found in the once-elegant districts bordering Henrietta Street, on the right bank of the Liffey. Its bleached, timeworn walls and stripped-down rooms are curiously more intriguing and evocative of the past than any immaculate refurbishment scheme could hope to be.

When the present owner bought the house it was a slum dwelling, its rooms subdivided by a maze of partitions. Now that these have been removed, a patchwork of faded colors decorates the walls of the beautifully proportioned reception rooms, which have retained their moldings, panelling, cornices, and other decorative details. The structure and function of the rooms is now revealed once more, and the original intention of the architecture, designed to impress the visitor with its splendor, is

again apparent.

This impression was created principally by the scale of the sparsely furnished rooms. Living conditions in the house today would not appear too unfamiliar to the original inhabitants, with the only heating being supplied by peat fires.

Seas, Lakes, and Rivers

Wherever you roam in Ireland, water is never far away. Its presence fills the air you breathe and lends the light its special quality. It also provides the key to the nature of the landscape and the distribution of the population.

It is to the Gulf Stream and the warm, rain-laden westerly winds from the Atlantic that Ireland owes its intense greenness and the abundance of subtropical vegetation that thrives in sheltered areas. Trees grow faster here than anywhere else in Europe, and the exceptionally gentle climate nurtures pastures which can be grazed year round, fostering a pastoral way of life that has survived to the present day.

Waterside buildings vary in their outward appearance and in their location according to function. Fishing harbors shelter fishermen's thatched cottages, their walls painted in pastel colors, while seaside resorts boast imposing Victorian villas, built to accommodate visitors and

A river in deepest Kerry (above).
The majestic Cliffs of Moher (opposite) on the west coast of County Clare.
Overleaf: Derryclare Lough, in the heart of Connemara.

families on holiday. Martello towers—including famously the one at Sandycove, immortalized by James Joyce in *Ulysses*—are circular fortifications dating from the Napoleonic Wars. Coastguards' cottages frequently have breathtaking sea views, while keeps and castles were built on lofty promontories which rendered them impregnable.

On an island which can be crossed by car in three hours, nobody lives very far from the sea. But Ireland is also strewn with over eight hundred lakes and rivers of significant size. It is rare to find a town or village without a river flowing either through or beside it. Indeed, rivers were frequently the focus of the original settlement, providing waters deep enough to build harbors, swift enough to power mills, or broad enough to carry merchandise.

Country people also chose to build their dwellings close to water for numerous reasons, apart from the obvious advantage of having one

of the necessities of life close at hand: the most fertile lands are often to be found flanking watercourses, for instance, and the rivers and lakes teem with a great variety of fish, including trout and salmon. And of course the prospect of a sheet of still water reflecting the sky and trees in its unruffled surface is restful and soothing to the spirit, a quality which in the past prompted the builders of the majority of Ireland's "big houses" to site them close to a lake or river. If a lake was lacking in the desired spot, they did not hesitate to create an artificial one in order to increase the charms of the parkland or gardens surrounding the house.

The most romantic of all Ireland's waterside dwellings are without doubt those to be found on the country's numerous islands: it is said that—without counting those in lakes or rivers—Ireland has as many islands as there are days in the year. Outstanding among these island residences is the sumptuous neoclassical mansion on the

The romantic landscape of Connemara (above) in the west of Ireland, a national park scattered with lakes and rivers.
Lough Tay (opposite) is a lake of exceptional beauty in the eastern county of Wicklow. It lies close to Glendalough, or the valley of two lakes, another area celebrated for its natural beauty.

island of Fota, set among a forest of rare trees. It is no coincidence that the majority of Ireland's most beautiful and fascinating houses stand close to water, the association of land and water being a source of eternal inspiration not only to painters and poets but also to architects.

About a hundred of Ireland's coastal islands, most of them lying a minimum of eight kilometers offshore, are inhabited. These island communities often have their own ancient and deeply rooted traditions and folklore, and the most remote of them, such as Tory Island off County Donegal, where the painter Derek Hill founded a school of primitive painting, shelter a way of life which has barely changed for centuries. On the Aran Islands—Inishmore, Inishmaan and Inisheer—Gaelic is still spoken.

People are now tending to drift away from the islands of Ireland, however, leaving them in the trusted hands of the lighthouse keepers and the birds.

Anyone who loves the sea will find countless opportunities in Ireland to experience the special charm of houses overlooking the waves. At Church Hill, on the shore of Gartan Lough in Donegal (these pages), the painter Derek Hill found inspiration for some of his finest canvases in the views of hills, lakes and sea, their colors ever changing and the light constantly varying with the season and the weather. He painted both here and on nearby Tory Island, where he bought another house and founded a school of primitive painting. The house overlooks a garden also designed by the painter. The entrance hall is decorated with souvenirs from his travels to Paris and in Russia and the Far East. The table came from a local secondhand shop; the walls are painted a dazzling blue derived from laundry blue. The drawing room with its palest lilac walls, bamboo furniture and Victorian

decor, has welcomed many famous visitors.
Derek Hill has bequeathed his house in Donegal and his collection of paintings to the state. Now it is open to all to admire its treasures, while the painter still visits his faithful housekeeper Gracie now and again in her brightly colored kitchen.

In the seventeenth century, Donegal—like the six counties of the present Northern Ireland—was subjected to the devastating policy of "plantation," by which rebellious provinces were subdued by having their lands confiscated and distributed to Scots planters and English colonists. Such was the sad fate suffered by this estate on the shores of Lough Swilly, whose waters were once plied by barges carrying goods to Derry. The present house, with its graceful facade looking out over the bay to a patchwork of fields beyond, dates from the eighteenth century. Following careful restoration, aided by fiscal reforms, it now makes an exceptionally warm and welcoming family house, as can be seen from its commodious kitchen.

In the early eighteenth century, Fota House was a hunting lodge on the island of Fota, in the confusion of land and water that never fails to bewitch visitors arriving at Cork by sea. The arboretum at Fota is famous not only for its rare trees but also for its aquatic plants thronging the lake shore. A magnificent specimen of Cryptomeria japonica spiralis (this page, right) is particularly admired by visitors to the gardens, now open to the public.

The most imposing room in Fota House, a popular destination for visitors to Cork and the surrounding area, is the splendid entrance hall (opposite left), embellished with columns in yellow imitation marble, with a collection of busts and urns from a country house in County Kildare.

The rooms of Fota House are now the setting for concerts, dinners, and

many other events attended by the inhabitants of Cork. Every room breathes its own special atmosphere, such as this bedroom (opposite below) with its lighted candles adding to the softness of its filtered light.

LIFE IN THE COUNTRY

A number of distinctive characteristics are quite particular to the Irish countryside. Habitations are extremely scattered, for instance, with many dwellings standing in isolation, frequently at some distance from the nearest road, rather than clustering in or around towns and villages. This phenomenon, which stands in such marked contrast to the customary approach in Britain and the rest of Europe, finds its explanation in Irish history, for these dwellings owe their loneliness to a very ancient tradition by which shepherds were expected to live in the midst of their fields.

It was a custom that was to be reinforced by the "plantation" system, particularly in the south and west of the country, where landowners owned vast tracts of land and housed their tenants in dwellings far removed fom each other.

Another striking feature of the Irish countryside, especially in the remotest areas, is its large numbers of abandoned cottages and farmhouses.

Some farms now have herds of goats, producing highly prized goats' cheese. This scene in County Carlow (opposite) is typical of the bogland landscapes to be found throughout Ireland. Overleaf: After the harvest, weighted ropes protect the haystacks from the wind.

Before the Great Famine, the population of the island as a whole stood at over eight million. Within three years, the potato blight had slashed the population by two million, a million souls having died of starvation, and another million having emigrated from Irish shores.

This decline was set to continue, largely as a result of the policies of the great landowners, who demanded exorbitant rents and evicted those unable to pay them, thus laying the foundations of future land wars. Unable to afford the risk of dividing their already reduced lands any further, smallholders resorted to putting off the marriage of their eldest sons and heirs until late in life, while other members of the family, seeing no future in Ireland, were driven to emigrate. While the population in general continued to fall, mass migrations to the towns and cities contributed to the depopulation of the countryside in particular. Even today, the total combined populations of Northern Ireland and the

Republic do not exceed five million inhabitants.

A further distinctive characteristic of rural Ireland is the stark disparity between imposing mansions and humble cottages, with very few houses of medium size in between. Generally speaking, rural habitations can be divided into two broad categories, with landowners' residences and other dwelling houses, whether sumptuous or simple, on the one hand, and the modest smallholdings and cottages of the peasantry on the other.

The gulf that separated the splendor of the first from the poverty of the second was an accurate reflection of the chasm that lay between the two unequal parts of the population: the native Irish peasantry and the Anglo-Normans, later to be joined by the planters and colonists who took over from the lords and Gaelic chieftains. The high walls and wooden fences erected to protect the estates of influential families are a marked peculiarity of the Irish countryside.

Stone walls trace long lines across the countryside, acting as windbreaks to retain the thin layer of arable soil grazed freely by cows, sheep, and horses. This characteristic feature of the Irish countryside is most common in the west, in County Clare, Connemara, and the Aran Islands.

The cottages and vernacular farm buildings of rural Ireland were traditionally built from local materials. Long after the Great Famine, the poorest peasants still lived in small huts with clay walls and thatched roofs. Brick was rare, with less basic buildings constructed of local stone. Walls were plastered and then painted or limewashed, and roofs were of slate or thatched with reeds, oats or rushes, according to what was available locally.

Building styles varied from region to region. Older farms and cottages invariably sit beautifully in their natural settings: the careful choice of position, the use of local materials and the Irish gift for adapting a dwelling to fit its environment are all factors which have contributed over the centuries to a perfect marriage of buildings and landscape. Sadly, this is no longer the case. The new houses springing up all over the Irish countryside, devoid of either soul and character, are now disfiguring a landscape which hitherto had remained virtually unspoilt.

Set in the midst of parklands grazed by Suffolk Cross sheep and shaded by beech trees, and looking out over undulating fields to the Blackstairs Mountains beyond, this solid little country house in County Wexford (opposite) is the epitome of the medium-sized dwellings of rural Ireland. Inside, the most arresting room—after the studio of the mistress of the house, a painter and decorative artist (left)—is the first-floor drawing room, which houses collections of period costumes, antique dolls and children's toys, an added attraction for visitors to this warm and colorful house.

As so often in Ireland, this house in County Wicklow is reached along a winding lane, tantalizing visitors by concealing it until they round the very last bend. The ancient trees among which it stands (opposite) have dated the house and provided clues to its long history, stretching back over centuries. Although relatively modest, it nevertheless betrays signs of grandeur, emphasized by the granite portico (left) added by the new owners.

The restraint of the façade is matched by an equally uncluttered interior, where the soft Irish light bathes rooms painted entirely in white.

No one would suspect that the remarkable neoclassical decorations which, together with its stucco ceilings, now embellish the house were not original. The work of the celebrated stucco-worker Robert West, they were in fact salvaged from a house in Dublin which has since

been demolished. Visitors to the house, moving from room to room on paths marked out in white canvas, can now admire them in this simple and harmonious setting.

COUNTRY HOUSES

In Ireland, the notion of the "big house" conjures up a host of images: lofty surrounding walls, long rutted avenues, hunting dogs bounding through a half-open gate, granite steps weathered by time, windows looking out over wooded parkland. An oblique term used to denote a landowner's residence, the expression is an essential part of the Irish vocabulary. While it is of course true that these "big houses" were often considerably larger than the dwellings of tenant farmers, the term may be applied equally well to a country house of modest size as to a vast pile.

Ireland possesses an astonishing number of these houses, built during the eighteenth and nineteenth centuries. The Burke's Peerage guide to Irish country houses alone mentions some two thousand, and there are thousands more besides. They are essentially the product of Ireland's history of invasion and pillage, which gave rise to a new breed of landowners. Before the defeat of Hugh O'Neill at Mellifont in 1603, most of Ireland

Castletown (above) in County Kilkenny is in the Palladian style, while Temple House (opposite) in County Sligo is a perfect example of Victorian building, its splendor bearing eloquent witness to the immense fortune of the merchant for whom it was built.

belonged to Catholics who were either Irish Celts or "Old English" Anglo-Normans. In 1660, land ownership underwent a fundamental shift, a massive change achieved by the combined expedients of confiscation, the plantation system and the ruthless policies of Oliver Cromwell, who famously professed his indifference as to whether the Irish people went "to Hell or to Connacht." A new class of Protestant landowners was thus born, whose powers were soon to be further reinforced by the penal laws aimed at subjugating the Catholics.

Most of Ireland's "big houses" were built over a period lasting barely a hundred years. Before 1690, virtually all major habitations were fortified; subsequently, as the social background became more stable, landowners abandoned their tower houses and set about building more comfortable residences. Of these early dwellings, many of which were little more than modest manorhouses, very few survive, most of them having been either demolished to make way for larger houses or transformed and renovated by owners anxious to keep up with the latest tastes in architecture.

Generally speaking, Irish architects adopted English fashions, which often underwent subtle modifications on the journey from one island to the other. It is to the resulting eccentricities of style that Irish architecture owes much of its charm. Fashions arrived late on Irish shores, and once there evolved at a slower pace, so that is not unusual to see two styles from successive periods juxtaposed in the same building.

Aristocratic families of slender means frequently dispensed with the services of an architect, or "artificer," choosing instead to employ simple builders. These took their inspiration from the building styles of neighboring houses, or relied on catalogues and books of architecture, sometimes with diverting results. Even the noblest residences of Ireland are by no means as large or pretentious as their English counter-

The Curragh, home of the Irish Derby, and the National Stud conspire to make County Kildare the land of horses par excellence. But throughout the country, stud farms, horse fairs, equestrian centers, and riding to hounds reveal the Irish passion for horses, which moreover make a significant contribution to the national economy.

parts. The various architectural styles of the era, such as Palladian or neoclassical, were moreover frequently adjusted to suit Irish tastes and pockets, thus giving rise to the singular character and charm of Ireland's country houses.

Among the most influential architects of the first half of the eighteenth century were Sir Edward Lovett Pearce, who introduced the Palladian style to Ireland, and his pupil Richard Castle. "Big houses" such as Castletown, Russborough and Carton are remarkable examples of the Palladian style.

Tall houses, less splendid and typically Irish, were buildings of three or four stories, almost as high as they were broad, and looking rather like latterday versions in the Georgian style of the ancient tower houses.

In an era when a gentleman's rank and influence were measured in terms of the size of his estate, the construction of an elegant residence became above all the outward sign of the owner's

social status. Building an imposing mansion, surrounding it with delightful gardens and parkland and embellishing it with the work of the most accomplished decorative artists were all means by which landowners could display not only their wealth but also their taste and refinement.

The tone was set by the English aristocracy, with their Anglo-Irish counterparts determined to follow suit despite the more limited resources at their disposal. Ironically, many of the proud possessors of these "big houses" lived far beyond their means. It was not uncommon for aristocratic families to be financially ruined by over-ambitious building projects, or to find themselves perennially unable to match their lifestyle to the splendor of the setting that they had created. The magnificence of these interiors was due largely to the skills of Irish decorative artists, and above all to a number of virtuoso stucco-workers, notably Robert West, the undisputed master of the rococo style, and Michael Stapleton and Richard Morrison, who excelled in the neoclassical style.

The building frenzy which produced such vast numbers of country houses abated in the wake of the Great Famine, gaining a fresh—if more

Wreathed in vegetation and topped by a characteristic fanlight, the Georgian door and door surround of this country house add a note of strong color to the Irish countryside.
Weathered granite steps (opposite) lead down to magnificent gardens sloping away gently to the white sands of Lough Swilly, in County Donegal.

moderate—lease of life during the Victorian period, only to peter out with the agricultural crisis of the 1880s. The Wyndham Act of 1903, by which the Senate was empowered to buy out the great estates in order to redistribute the land to the Irish peasantry, finally set the seal on the pampered lifestyle of Ireland's wealthy landowners.

A number of "big houses"—though not as many as is commonly imagined—were burnt down during the civil war which ravaged Ireland in the 1920s. Many more were simply abandoned or demolished by farmers more interested in land than in architecture, and without the means of maintaining buildings of such importance.

The reaction of the Irish people to these great residences has gradually changed over the years, the deep-rooted antipathy they inspired at the time of the Great Famine giving way to a relative indifference, to be replaced only recently by an increasing concern for their future. Recognition that they form part of Ireland's heritage, frequently sheltering superb examples of the work of Irish artists and craftsmen, is now—finally—accompanied by a realization that they are in themselves works of art in danger of being lost forever.

The finest of Ireland's Palladian villas, Castletown (these pages) nestles in gently rolling hills overlooking the Suir valley in County Kilkenny. This elegant residence, decorated by one of the most celebrated of Irish stucco-workers, has survived the passing centuries virtually intact. The parterres of French inspiration were laid out in about 1910. Their upkeep, originally entrusted to a staff of twenty-four gardeners, has now devolved on the present owner himself, who has replaced the former floral displays in the box compartments with more practical gravel. Castletown is privately owned, but visitors are welcome at Russborough, another jewel of the Palladian style, which lies a mere thirty kilometers from Dublin in County Wicklow.

Ballyorney House in County Wicklow is among the most spectacular of Ireland's country houses, with a drawing room (opposite) embellished with one of the finest examples of eighteenth-century stucco decor. Reproduced from a fragment taken from a now-demolished house in O'Connell Street, Dublin, this masterpiece was carefully dismantled and stored in a city office in order to safeguard it from vandalism.

Newbridge House, near Dublin (right) remained in the same family for two and a half centuries before being bought by the city corporation, which opened its collections of furniture, painting and other objets d'art to the public. The gallery that served as an antechamber to the great drawing room is decorated with classical statues, brought back from their travels by the family that built the house.

The impressive Portland stone chimneypiece in the entrance hall at Newbridge House (opposite) bears the coat of arms of the family that built the house, and in whose hands it remained for two hundred and fifty years. This ancestral home, once the scene of glittering receptions, has a lived-in charm not often found in houses open to the public. In the spectacular Red Drawing Room, a console table and mirror (above) bear witness to the exuberance of the Georgian era. Today this room houses part of the magnificent collection of seventeenth- and eighteenth-century paintings amassed by the original owners and their descendants.

The main facade (right) has remained virtually unaltered since the house was built. The original house, laid out on a classic rectangular plan, was relatively modest in scale, and an imposing wing was added to the back of the building in the eighteenth century. One of the most intriguing rooms at Newbridge is undoubtedly the "Museum of Curiosities," created in the late nineteenth century and believed to be unique in the British Isles.

The furnishings and layout of Temple House (these pages) in County Sligo, the land of Yeats, remain very much as they were conceived by its Hong Kong-resident owner in 1863.

Its ninety rooms are now enjoyed by paying guests, who are greeted in the hall, with its handsome pale sandstone staircase, by a gallery of family portraits, hunting trophies and glass cases containing stuffed birds mounted by a well-known Dublin taxidermist. The windows of the south facade provide glimpses of the silvery waters of a lake and the imposing ruins of an eighteenth-century castle. An array of wellington boots and fishing tackle await the visitor, who may either stroll through the Italianate gardens or go fishing for pike.

In their faded glory, the window hangings, carpets and mirrors of the drawing room (opposite), all specially designed for the house in the late nineteenth century, are eloquent survivors of the splendor of former times. While a number of concessions have been made to modern standards of comfort (the original heating system consumed up to one and a half tons of wood daily), the period four-poster beds, the drawing room with its covers protecting antique silk upholstery and the dining room with its handsome English furniture all combine to imbue the atmosphere with an authentically Victorian aroma (indeed all other

perfumes are discouraged by the owner, who is allergic to them!) Visitors now come to Temple House to fish for pike, hunt woodcock on the estate, or savor dishes prepared with produce from the kitchen garden.

HIDDEN PATHS

Ireland is crammed with secret places. Head off across the fields from any road, and you are bound to come upon unexpected landscapes. In this land of constantly changing scenery, particularly in the west and along the coast, every twist and turn in the road is likely to conceal a surprise. The next bend may reveal the ruins of a medieval tower, a sandy cove fringed by cliffs or a tranquil lake sheltering fish and wild birds, or it may lead past an abandoned stone cottage or a diminutive Georgian country house, half-hidden by a curtain of trees. Heading off the beaten track is a virtually infallible way of discovering corners that are as beautiful as they are out of the way.

In one sense, the majority of the houses described in this book could be described as secret places, for—remote as they are, and concealed behind high walls or at the end of unfrequented tracks—they all have the secluded air of some kind of hideaway.

This remote spot above Laragh in County Wicklow (above) shelters a water garden laid out on the hillside and embellished with granite steps.
A Gothic Revival hunting lodge in the same county (opposite) sits quite naturally in its romantic setting.

A knowledge of this network of hidden byways has for many years formed part of Irish folklore, for in order to overcome the enemy or elude him, it was sometimes sufficient to take to the labyrinth of tracks known only to the natives, threading a path across treacherous boglands. Should you get carried away with following the twists and turns of a tangle of tiny roads or admiring the splendor of the Wicklow Mountains, it is still quite possible to get completely lost in the countryside within fifty kilometers of Dublin.

Ireland is a country offering peace and repose to the soul, a paradise for those in search of solitude. The entire island contains fewer inhabitants than any single one of the world's great cities, and the roads are virtually empty. The least populated country in Europe, the whole island has a population amounting to a mere five and a half million, as compared to the United Kingdom's fifty-five million.

Rural Ireland's many secluded houses concealed in unexpected spots offer the charm of delightful hideaways far from the cares of the world. These qualities of seclusion, tranquillity, and natural beauty are three of the country's greatest assets, making it a perfect haven for lovers of solitude.

One family is thus able to contemplate views of the mountains around Laragh from the windows of its inaccessible hillside retreat, less than an hour's drive from Dublin. And it would be hard to imagine a more romantic setting than the windswept cliffs overlooking the Atlantic on which Tomi Ungerer's house is perched. The possibility of stumbling across such an idyllic hideaway is one of Ireland's most powerful lures.

It was in Kerry, after exploring miles of remote byways, that the novelist Benoîte Groult came upon her few acres of moorland: "It all started with images which I thought were insignificant . . . A black-and-white dog setting off down

Heather on moorland in County Mayo (above). With its views of the distant mountains of Knockmealdown and Comeragh, this house in County Cork (opposite), parts of which are probably over four hundred years old, is now the tranquil retreat of a well-known actor.

a lane glistening with rain which apparently led nowhere. ...And that unforgettable Aer Lingus commercial showing a ridiculous little track rambling between grassy meadows enclosed by dry stone walls, running alongside other meandering walls, leading to yet more and more walls, thousands of walls, dividing the land into tiny squares and vanishing into the mountains, protecting what, against whom? And that inspired saying: 'Here the roads were laid out by donkeys, not engineers!'"

The Irish think of their country as a forsaken land. From the "Flight of the Earls" in the seventeenth century to Joyce's "quiet exile" and the emigration of huge numbers of young people, continuing to this day, Ireland has always been the island that people leave behind. But the green fields of Erin are also a restful sanctuary, a paradise for sports enthusiasts and a haven of peace for anyone wishing to escape the tumult of twentieth-century life.

In the most remote parts of
Ireland there can still be
found clusters of small house
known as clochàns. The one
shown on these pages, on the
west coast of County Cork,
was probably abandoned
during the great rural
exodus of the 1950s and
1960s. Built on a treeless,
wind-lashed promontory
jutting out into the Atlantic,
its only link with the world
outside is a meandering
track.
From his window the
designer Tomi Ungerer, who
lives here with his family,
looks out over the bay and
the promontory beside it. His
wife has converted part of
the hamlet into a sheep
farm. Within the carefully
restored house, the principal
feature of the decor is its use
of natural materials, with
stripped wood
complementing traditional
Irish pottery.

This romantic Gothic Revival retreat (these pages) was built originally as a hunting lodge and used for only a few months of the year. It retains its original function to this day, welcoming members of the public in organized parties to hunt deer, grouse, and other game. Fires are lit in all the fireplaces before dawn, using peat stored in great wooden tubs hooped in copper (opposite right). In the dining room (left), traditional harps arranged around the Irish hunting table form part of the owner's collection of musical instruments. The harpsichord with upright case (oppposite left) dates from the eighteenth century; a similar piece by the same maker can be seen in the National Museum in Dublin.

THE ROMANCE OF COTTAGES

The traditional rural houses which are so much a part of the landscape and folklore of Ireland are increasingly a vanishing feature of the Irish countryside. So romantic to our eyes, with their thatched roofs and limewashed walls, they are in fact lucky survivors of a history fraught with dangers.

The architecture of these long, low buildings made of local materials was shaped by long-held though now increasingly forgotten traditions. Two principal considerations determined the initial choice of site: the availability of fresh water and the need for protection from the wind. Thus all these cottages were built near springs or streams, with the exact position—in Donegal at any rate—being settled by the custom of throwing a hat into the air on a windy day and seeing where it came down.

Such cottages are to be found all over the Irish countryside, except in the mountains and boglands. In the most remote regions, it is also

A cottage at the foot of Croagh Patrick (opposite), the famous place of pilgrimage in County Mayo from which St Patrick is said to have banished all snakes from Ireland.
Reeds (above) are traditionally used as thatch.
Overleaf: A traditional cottage at Doolin in County Clare.

still possible to find surviving examples of small hamlets known as *clochàns*, each generally inhabited in former times by a single extended family living and working as a cooperative.

These vernacular dwellings exist in many different forms, needless to say. Some were clustered around centers of common interest—the mill or the castle, for instance—and gradually expanded to become villages, while others were built by great landowners to house their tenants. Both these categories, inspired no doubt by the model villages then in vogue in England, were characterized by an architectural style which was considerably more elaborate than that of isolated cottages. Adare in County Limerick, with its saffron-colored cottages, and Caledon in County Tyrone are two interesting examples of estate villages constructed around a landowner's residence. In numerous other towns and villages dating from the eighteenth and nineteenth centuries, cottages and modest houses hang on the

fringes of the more luxurious houses of merchants and notables, gathered together in the center. These rows of cottages lining the streets of towns and villages, each painted a different color, are one of the typical sights of Ireland.

At the entrance to the great estates there sometimes still stand gatekeepers' lodges, distinctive in style and often resembling in miniature the architectural style of the "big houses" they served. Other small buildings designed for specific purposes include toll-houses, still to be found strung out on major roads, and lock-keepers' cottages on the canals.

A number of wealthy nineteenth-century landowners had cottages built for their own amusement, in which to enjoy life's simple pleasures. These romantic confections, carefully positioned in the most picturesque spot on the estate, were generally in the Gothic Revival style then in vogue. Georgian and Victorian hunting and fishing lodges, meanwhile, were substantial-

The villages of County Kilkenny (above), one of the least visited parts of the country, have a special charm, with their carefully limewashed storybook cottages.
In Glen Irragh, County Galway (opposite), peat dug in spring is left to dry throughout the summer before being stored inside to serve as fuel for the winter.

ly superior in comfort to the huts in which much of the peasantry lived.

At their finest, the rural dwellings of Ireland are the embodiments of the architectural style particular to their region. The materials used, the choice of architectural motifs and the skill of the builders, with their instinctive feeling for proportion and their talent for blending their work harmoniously into the surrounding environment, have all helped to ensure that these cottages sit perfectly in the natural landscape.

Abandoned for the most part by their original occupants, some of these cottages are now enjoying a second lease of life as holiday homes, and new holiday villas built on the model of traditional cottages have enjoyed a great success. The Dallas-style bungalows which have supplanted cottages in rural areas are a travesty, however, and a miserable substitute for the simple perfection of the original.

Utter simplicity is the
hallmark of the interior of
this cottage at Dunquin
(left), "the last parish before
America," with limewashed

walls, a bare concrete floor and peat burning in the fireplace. Looking out over the sea and the Blasket Islands on one side and the wild Kerry countryside on the other, it is a part-time retreat for a Dublin painter who exhibits in London and New York. Hanging in a window embrasure (opposite above) is a painting showing a scene from the life of fishermen on the Blasket Islands, off the coast of Kerry.

This small, rustic cottage (right) on the fringes of an oak wood sloping gently down to banks of the River Kenmare, also in County Kerry, now makes a delightful holiday home.

One of the finest sights in Northern Ireland used to be the flax fields in bloom, with vast sheets of sky-blue flowers undulating and rippling in the wind. This was the raw material of the famous Irish linen industry, now fast disappearing. At Marybrook Mill in County Down, however, this traditional skill is being revived: around the house, now carefully restored, are now a working mill supplying flour to the local baker, a weaving shed for the flax being cultivated on the estate once more, and a farm. Thus an important part of traditional rural life in Ulster is gradually being brought back to life. The vertical bars on the fireplace at Marybrook (left) indicate that it was used to burn the sloughs that sheathed the flax fibers. The nineteenth-century mill buildings were still intact when one of the directors of the National Trust for Ireland decided to undertake their restoration. The millwheel at Marybrook still turns today (below), working the machinery that crushes the linen threads.

IRISH CASTLES

Of all the different types of dwelling to be found in these shores, it is of course the castles of Ireland—in all their tremendous variety—which exert the the most powerful fascination. From dour medieval keeps guarding great swathes of land to small and delightful mock Gothic Victorian affairs, all evoke the country's rich history.

The whole story of Ireland is present in these walls, which stand now as testimony to the different eras in which they were built. The earliest fortified sites, known as *duns*, were Iron Age hillforts surrounded by walls and ditches, which found variants in bastions projecting from defensive outer walls or dominating promontories, and in *crannogs*, or lake villages. The remains of many of these fortified sites can still be seen today.

The castles which are most familiar to us were built by the Anglo-Normans following the invasion of 1169. The earliest were wooden keeps built on mounds—many of which are also still

Adare is one of the most picturesque villages in the whole of Ireland. Adare Manor (opposite) is now a hotel where guests come to fish, hunt, play golf, or simply stroll in the superb gardens.
Markree Castle (above) in County Sligo is another fine residence skilfully transformed into a welcoming hotel.

discernible today—and surrounded by ditches and palisades, but having swiftly invaded three-quarters of the country, the Norman conquerors set about consolidating their position by building a wave of authentic fortresses.

These Norman citadels vary greatly in scale and sophistication, from simple stone keeps, generally surrounded by a defensive wall, to vast complexes protected by elaborate defences. Built on high ground from which they could command the surrounding countryside or in positions of strategic importance, these ancient strongholds are today characterized above all by the exceptional beauty of their settings.

The greatest concentration of Ireland's castles is to be found in the southwest of the island, while the most splendid lie in the Dublin area. "Here a grandeur more imposing than anywhere else has provided grottoes and obelisks, temples and waterfalls, and terraced gardens. Often nature, that eminent landscape architect, arranges her views of hills and mountains, valleys, lakes, and rivers as an extension to their beauty," as Anne Pons wrote in her book on Ireland. A ruined tower on a hilltop is a typical sight in Counties Limerick, Cork, Galway, and Tipperary.

The sheer numbers of castles built in Ireland—some three thousand between the twelfth and the seventeenth centuries—is an indication in itself of their importance in former times.

The defensive architecture that prevailed throughout the Middle Ages assumed a variety of forms. Members of the ruling classes typically lived in tower houses of three, four or even five stories, with the living quarters elevated to the top floor. More elaborate fortresses were equipped with the full gamut of defences, including barbicans, drawbridges, watchtowers and loopholes, through which in time of war projectiles and scalding liquids could be showered on their attackers.

The gardens of Powerscourt House (above), at the foot of the Wicklow Mountains, are among the finest in Europe. Closer to Dublin, Luttrellstown (opposite) boasts a Gothic Revival facade complete with turrets and crenellations.
Overleaf: The castle-hotel of Ballynahinch is an ideal place to stay for salmon-fishing.

Towers and castles continued to be built throughout the sixteenth and seventeenth centuries, a period of tremendous upheaval in Irish history. The colonists who took over Irish lands at this time also built fortified dwellings, which in Ulster are still known as "plantation castles."

Towards the end of the seventeenth century, however, minor aristocrats began increasingly to abandon their castles in order to build more comfortable dwellings, often close to or even adjoining the older construction. Palladian and neoclassical architecture were now *de rigueur*, and castles were soon considered hopelessly old-fashioned.

Then, inevitably, fashions changed, and by about 1790 castles came to be viewed as the epitome of the Gothic style, which remained in vogue throughout the Romantic period. These new residences in the medieval style offered a considerably greater degree of comfort than the real thing

had done, however. Frequently, their architects merely embellished them with machicolations, turrets and fan vaults in imitation of their medieval ancestors. Numerous Georgian houses were thus endowed with towers and crenellations in order to be brought up to date in the Gothic style. Elsewhere, meanwhile, gracious Gothic Revival dwellings began to rise from genuinely ancient foundations, as at Luttrellstown, near Dublin, one of the finest examples of this type.

The Victorian period also displayed a great enthusiasm for medieval architecture, with Gothic coming back into fashion with a vengeance at the expense of neoclassicism, now abandoned as a style. This passion for the castles of the Middle Ages assumed considerable proportions, and architects began to employ a decorative vocabulary heavily inspired by medieval defensive architec-

The arboretum at Johnstown Castle (above) in County Wexford, ancestral home of the Kennedy family, is dedicated to the former American president and named after him.
Ruins reflected in the River Maigue at Adare (opposite). Vestiges such as these hold clues to Ireland's history and its faith.

ture, even to the extent of building sham keeps and watchtowers.

Ireland's great wealth of castles is one of the finest manifestations of its architectural heritage. While some are now abandoned and in ruins, others are now protected from further deterioration by the Ministry of Public Works, and some are still inhabited today. Many are now open to the public, some have been converted into museums, and a few are even hotels, where guests may experience the splendor of former centuries while at the same time enjoying modern standards of comfort.

Yet others are available for hire, including Luttrellstown, which served as the setting for the film *The Knights of the Round Table.* The former stables have even been converted into holiday cottages, popular with golfers attracted by the golf course laid out within the grounds of the immense estate.

Castle Leslie (these pages), at Glaslough, County Monaghan, was built on a site overlooking the waters of the lake in the late nineteenth century. At that time, the Leslies were one of Ireland's greatest landowning families, and around their mansion they built an estate village to house their tenants. Nowadays, the gardens are leased to a plant nursery and the stables house a riding center. The house is open to the public, and teas are served in the conservatory.

The most striking feature of the stately entrance hall (opposite left) is its mosaic floor depicting doves of peace (a copy of a mosaic at Pompeii).

At the foot of the service stairs (opposite below), serried ranks of no fewer than twenty-nine bells recall the days when there were sufficient numbers of servants to be able to recognize and respond to the different chime of each one of them.

The fittings and services at Castle Leslie—the finest products of Victorian engineering skills—put it in the forefront of technical advances of the time. An enormous boiler heated the reception rooms and the conservatory, filled at that time with exotic plants. It now contains a copy of Nero's throne (right), brought back from one of his numerous Italian journeys by John Leslie, the fourth baronet.

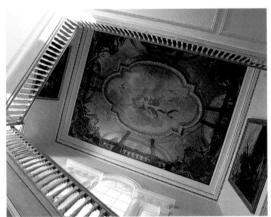

Luttrellstown Castle (these pages) has a complex architectural history: originally a medieval castle, it was transformed successively into a neoclassical country house, a Gothic Revival castle and a Tudor mansion, before returning finally to the Gothic style, as can be seen in the entrance hall (opposite left), with its fine Chippendale-style mirror. The great staircase (opposite above) was redesigned in the eighteenth century to suit contemporary tastes. Luttrellstown's legendary comfort and hospitality are nowadays enjoyed by conferences and private receptions. The bedrooms have been fitted out with bathrooms, some of which are virtuoso examples of the Victorian art of sanitation (opposite below). The dining room (right) is decorated with a ceiling painting by the Dutch painter Jacob de Witt.

Ireland is a land of birds: among other species, Dublin Bay attracts wild geese, curlews, puffins, and gulls. On the island of Lambay to the north of the city, now a bird sanctuary sheltering rare species, the celebrated English architect Edwin Lutyens transformed an ancient fort into an architectural masterpiece (these pages), using the island's prized grey-green porphyry.

The charm of the gardens, also designed by Lutyens, derives principally from its different vistas (above left). Lutyens also designed the furniture, including this four-poster bed (far left) which stands in a bedroom heated by a fine porphyry chimneypiece.

In the drawing room, birds' eggs collected by the owner are put on display (below left).

VISITOR'S GUIDE

Some of the many charms of Ireland—green moorland and meadows, magnificent historic mansions, intimate cottages—are explored in these pages. The following list of useful addresses includes not only those places mentioned in the book which are open to the public (with cross-references to pages on which photographs appear), but also a selection of other sites which merit a visit by virtue of their beauty and their historic or artistic importance.

As Ireland possesses such a wealth of outstanding places to stay, the list concentrates on organizations specializing in a particular type of accommodation, with the addition of a few hotels of prestige.

To telephone Ireland from abroad, dial 00, followed by 353 for the Republic of Ireland, followed by the area code and number. When telephoning Northern Ireland from outside the United Kingdom, dial 00 followed by 44.

USEFUL ADDRESSES FOR BOOKING ACCOMMODATION

IRISH TOURIST BOARD
(BORD FÁILTE)
Baggot Street Bridge
Dublin 2
Tel.: (1) 602 4000

NORTHERN IRELAND TOURIST BOARD (BELFAST)
St Anne's Court
59 North Street
Tel.: (1232) 231221

NORTHERN IRELAND TOURIST BOARD (DUBLIN)
16 Nassau Street
Tel.: (1) 679 1851

A small selection from the many brochures produced by these organizations:

HERITAGE ISLAND
Dublin, fax: (1) 260 0058
A guide to Ireland's rich heritage, including not only castles and country houses, national parks, caves etc., but also national resources such as linen, beer, whiskey, and stud farms.

THE HIDDEN IRELAND
Dublin, tel.: (1) 662 7166
A selection of fine private houses in magnificent settings where guests in search of authenticity are accorded a warm family welcome. Our particular favourites (all on lakeshores) are *Ardanamona*, Co. Donegal; *Enniscoe House*, Co. Mayo and *Delphi Lodge*, Co. Galway.

ELEGANT IRELAND
Dublin, tel.: (1) 475 1665
Luxurious and spectacular listed buildings, including a fifteenth-century tower house on the River Shannon, a Gothic Revival castle, a Georgian mansion, a former presbytery, and a castle on the shores of Lough Erne redecorated by David Hicks.

For more modest but equally charming accommodation, see the *Bed and Breakfast* guides, containing dozens of addresses for each county and illustrated in color (based in Ballyshannon, Co. Donegal, tel.: (72) 51377); *Coast and Country* and *Village Inn Hotels of Ireland*, offering a selection of small traditional hotels (based in Dublin, tel.: (1) 295 8900); *Ireland Self-Catering Guide*, an illustrated catalogue of the cottages of your dreams (based in Cork, tel.: (21) 273251); and *Irish Farmhouse Holidays* (based in Limerick, tel.: (61) 400700). Other hotel associations offer small and select lists in *Manor House Hotels* (based in Dublin, tel.: (1) 295 8900) and *Friendly Homes of Ireland* (also in Dublin, tel.: (1) 668 6463).

HOTELS

A number of Ireland's country houses have now become prestigious hotels, some with restaurants of considerable repute. They make a splendid setting for afternoon tea.

ADARE MANOR
Adare, Co. Limerick
Tel.: (61) 396566 *(p. 76)*

This immense Victorian mansion in one of Ireland's most picturesque—and most visited—villages is now a luxurious hotel which attracts an international clientele of fishermen, hunters, and golfers.

ARBUTUS LODGE
Martenotte
Cork
Tel.: (21) 501237
Just outside Cork, in the middle of a garden of arbutus trees which have given their name to this hotel, this residence offers a superb view over the river. The food is excellent, specializing in fish and game.

ASSOLAS COUNTRY HOUSE
Kanturk
Co. Cork
Tel.: (29) 50015
This country residence beside a river seems to have stepped out of a fairy-tale. The owners take great leasure in welcoming visitors into this their family home which is furnished with antiques.

BALLYMALOE HOUSE
Shanagarry, Middleton,
Co. Cork
Tel.: (21) 652531
Within this handsome Georgian
house—and adjacent to one of
the country's most highly
reputed cookery schools—is one
of the finest restaurants in
Ireland.

BALLYNAHINCH CASTLE
Recess, Connemara, Co. Galway
Tel.: (95) 31006 (pp. 80–1)
A paradise for golf and fishing
enthusiasts, this historic
mansion lies in the heart of
Connemara, one of the most
beautiful regions in the whole of
Ireland.

CLARENCE HOTEL
6 Wellington Quay
Dublin
Co. Dublin
Tel.: (1) 670 9000
Recently restored this hotel on
the banks of the Liffey is
certainly the most elegant in the
city, and possesses an
unpretentious charm.

HUNTER'S HOTEL
Newrathbridge Rathnew
Co. Wicklow
Tel.: (404) 40106
Situated to the south of Dublin,
this eighteenth-century

posthouse, now a riverside
country hotel offers a pleasant
retreat, and a delightful
restaurant, surrounded by a
wonderful garden.

LONGUEVILLE HOUSE
Mallow, Co. Cork
Tel.: (22) 47156
Set in green countryside, this
Georgian house offers elegant
rooms furnished with period
furniture.

MARKREE CASTLE
Collooney, Co. Sligo
Tel.: (71) 67800 (p.77)
Sumptuous interiors and
attractive gardens distinguish
this country residence offering a
stylish welcome and exquisite
cuisine.

MOYGLARE MANOR
Maynooth
Co. Dublin
Tel.: (1) 628 6351
A manor house which has been
restored to its Georgian
splendor, Moyglare's rich
decors alone are worth a visit.
The guest rooms are also a
delight.

SHELBOURNE HOTEL
27 St Stephen's Green
Dublin 2
Tel.: (1) 676 6471

In its incomparable position in
the heart of old Dublin, the
hotel offers an immensely
elegant welcome, service, and
cuisine. The bar is well stocked
with Irish whiskeys as well as
ryes and bourbons.

TEMPLE HOUSE
Ballymote, Co. Sligo
Tel.: (71) 83329 (pp. 44; 56–7)
The owners welcome visitors to
this handsome and typically
Victorian house. A delicious
dinner in the dining room with
its fine English furniture is a
moment to savor.

HISTORIC HOUSES

From among all the
manorhouses and castles one
can visit we have chosen to list
the most intimate, even if some
have been converted into
museums or hotels. They
provide a wonderful insight
into Ireland's tradition
of decorative arts.

BANTRY HOUSE
Bantry, Co. Cork
Tel.: (27) 50047
A superb eighteenth-century
mansion set in beautiful
Italianate gardens overlooking
Bantry Bay. It houses
exceptional collections of

furniture and works of art,
as well as six guest rooms.

BERKELEY FOREST HOUSE
New Ross, Co. Wexford
Tel.: (51) 21361 (pp. 40–1)
A beautiful family home housing
fine collections of eighteenth-
and nineteenth-century dolls,
toys, and costumes.

CASTLE COOLE
Enniskillen, Co. Fermanagh
Northern Ireland
Tel.: (1365) 322690
This Palladian mansion is one of
the National Trust's finest
treasures. The Regency drawing
room with its mirrors and
woodcarvings and the sumptuous
reception hall created for George
IV are not to be missed.

CASTLE LESLIE
Glaslough, Co. Monaghan
Tel.: (47) 88109 (pp. 84–5)
This handsome Victorian
mansion, which in its heyday
welcomed so many celebrated
guests, now makes its rooms
available to visitors. The
conservatory makes a highly
romantic setting for tea.

DUBLIN WRITERS' MUSEUM
18–19 Parnell Square North,
Dublin
Tel.: (1) 872 2077

Jonathan Swift, Oscar Wilde,
Bernard Shaw, James Joyce,
Samuel Beckett, W.B. Yeats,
J.M. Synge and Brendan Behan
are among the writers whose
manuscripts, letters, and first
editions can be seen in this pair
of beautiful eighteenth-century
houses.

DUNKATHEL
Glanmire, Co. Cork
Tel.: (21) 821014
The former residence of a
wealthy merchant, this house
contains a fine example of
Italian stucco-work as well as an
extremely rare barrel organ
dating from 1880, which still
entertains visitors.

EMO COURT
Emo, Co. Laois
Tel.: (502) 26110
Emo Court is famous for its fine
neoclassical facade which looks
out over gardens leading down
to the lake. Its architect, James
Gandon, was also responsible
for much of the neoclassical
architecture in Dublin. The
rotunda, topped by a cupola
inspired by the Pantheon in
Rome, is one of the most
spectacular rooms in Ireland.

GLEBE HOUSE AND GALLERY
Church Hill

Letterkenny, Co. Donegal
Tel.: (74) 37071 *(p. 28)*
The house is home to the art collection presented to the state by the celebrated painter Derek Hill, as well as to three hundred other works by well-known twentieth-century artists.

GLIN CASTLE
Glin, Co. Limerick
Tel.: (68) 34173
This long white building with its neoclassical decor on the banks of the River Shannon makes a perfect setting for a remarkable collection of Irish eighteenth-century mahogany furniture. Visitors may come to dine, stay overnight or even hire the entire castle. The colorful gardens are open to the public.

LUGGALA ESTATE
Roundwood, Co. Wicklow
Tel.: (1281) 8424 *(pp. 59; 64–5)*
A romantic hunting lodge which may be hired for receptions. Hunting parties are still organized on a regular basis.

LUTTRELLSTOWN CASTLE
Castle Knock, Dublin 15
Tel.: (1) 808 9900 *(pp. 79; 86–7)*
This originally thirteenth-century castle with its Gothic Revival entrance hall and superb eighteenth-century staircase may

IRELAND'S LOVELIEST LANDSCAPES

Among all the natural riches of Ireland, here are some of its most spectacular landscapes, traveling from north to south.

THE GIANT'S CAUSEWAY, Co. Antrim
Thousands of hexagonal columns of black basalt plunging into the sea make one of the most thrilling landscapes to be seen anywhere in the world.

LOUGH ERNE, Co. Fermanagh
The heart of Ireland's region of loughs (lakes), many with majestic mansions set on their shores.

DONEGAL
A superb region less visited by tourists than the counties of the southwest, and offering three outstanding sights: *Bloody Foreland* on the coast, so named because of the color of the rocks; *Glencolumbkille*, with its Folk Village showing the history of life in the area through three traditional cottages dating from 1720, 1820, and 1920; and finally the *Slieve League*, with its breathtaking views of the *Cliffs of Bunglass*.

GALWAY
Galway boasts the *Connemara* national park, (a magnificent region of mountains, lakes and streams) and the *Aran Islands* in Galway Bay, with their drystone walls etching intricate patterns across the countryside, celebrated by J.M. Synge and the film director Flaherty.

CLARE
Here the rocky landcapes of the Burren, with their mixture of Mediterranean and alpine flora, culminate in the towering *Cliffs of Moher*.

KERRY
In this most visited part of Ireland, the *Dingle Peninsula* should not be missed, with *Slea Head* and the *Blasket Islands*, the lakes of *Killarney*, the astonishing *Gap of Dunloe*, and finally the *Ring of Kerry*, and the *Skellig Islands*.

CORK
Here, the remote, wild beauty of *Mizen Head*, the southernmost peninsula of Ireland, has proved irresistible to many foreigners who have chosen to settle there.

be hired exclusively for private receptions.

MALAHIDE CASTLE
Malahide, Co. Dublin
Tel.: (1) 846 2184
Among the many treasures in this medieval castle to the north of Dublin are a collection of eighteenth-century Irish furniture, fine rococo plasterwork and an oak-panelled drawing room. Just as delightful is the recently created garden.

MARY BROOK MILLS
Raleagh Road, Crossgar,
Co. Down
Northern Ireland
Tel.: (1396) 830173 *(pp. 74–5)*
The rustic charm of this ancestral home with its mill and weaving shed recalls the bucolic nature of traditional rural life in the Six Counties. Go when the flax fields are in flower.

NEWBRIDGE HOUSE
Donabate, Co. Dublin
Tel.: (1) 843 6534 *(pp. 53–5)*
The discreet charms of this elegant country seat and family home include the red drawing room, a superb example of the Georgian style, and the famous Museum of Curiosities, founded at the end of the nineteenth century.

NUMBER TWENTY-NINE
29 Lower Fitzwilliam Street,
Dublin 2
Tel.: (1) 702 6165
In this handsome restored
Georgian house, visitors may
get a taste the luxurious and
cosseted lifestyle of the Dublin
bourgeoisie in the late eighteenth
century.

ORMOND CASTLE
Carrick-on-Suir, Co. Tipperary
Tel.: (51) 640787
The facade of this castle not far
from Shannon is a perfect
example of the Elizabethan
style, while the Long Gallery has
extremely fine stucco
decorations.

ROTHE HOUSE MUSEUM
Parliament Street, Kilkenny
Tel.: (56) 22893
This Tudor house built for a
wealthy merchant is now owned
by the local archeological
association, which stages
exhibitions of traditional
costumes and accessories.

RUSSBOROUGH HOUSE
Blessington, Co. Wicklow
Tel.: (45) 865239
One of the most outstanding
Palladian villas in Ireland,
Russborough is famous for the
exuberant stucco ceilings of its

drawing room, library and
music room, and for the
sumptuousness of its decor,
featuring panelling, elaborate
chimneypieces, etc.

STROKESTOWN PARK HOUSE
Strokestown, Co. Roscommon
Tel.: (78) 33013
At the end of the widest street in
Ireland, a Gothic-style arch
marks the entrance to this
Palladian villa, which includes
vestiges of the original fortified
house. The stableyards contain
the Irish Famine Museum,
dedicated to the great tragedy
of the 1840s.

SWISS COTTAGE
Ardfinnan Road, Cahir,
Co. Tipperary
Tel.: (52) 41144
In the early nineteenth century,
the Duke of Glengall
commissioned this thatched
cottage from the architect John
Nash in which to indulge in the
pleasures of rustic life *à la*
Marie-Antoinette. Now owned
by the state, it has been restored
under the direction of Sybil
Connolly and is now a museum.
A tea room is also available.

SYBIL CONNOLLY'S HOUSE
71 Merrion Square, Dublin W2
Tel.: (1) 676 7281

The beautiful Georgian house of
Sybil Connolly, the famous
stylist whose clients included
Tiffany, contains a small
showroom and gift shop.
The pretty garden is also open
to visitors.

GARDENS

ANNES GROVE GARDENS
Castletownroche, Co. Cork
Tel.: (22) 26145
These gardens laid out in
natural fashion on the banks
of a river contain, among other
plants of interest, magnolias
of remarkable size.

**BALLYMALOE COOKERY
SCHOOL GARDENS**
Shanagarry, Middleton,
Co. Cork
Tel.: (21) 646785
The gardens of this world-
famous cookery school contain a
kitchen garden, an orchard and
a delightful herb garden, as well
as a Celtic maze.

BUTTERSTREAM GARDEN
Trim, Co. Meath
Tel.: (46) 36017
The most imaginative
contemporary garden in
Ireland, according to *House and
Garden*, offering teas and plants
for sale.

**DUNLOE CASTLE
HOTEL GARDENS**
Beaufort, Killarney, Co. Kerry
Tel.: (64) 44111
Camellias, roses, magnolias,
and rhododendrons flourish
here among a number of rare
species brought from around
the world.

FOTA ARBORETUM
Fota Estate, Carrigtwohill,
Co. Cork
Tel.: (21) 812728 *(pp.32–3)*
The arboretum on this island in
Cork Bay is famous for its rare
species, trees, and shrubs from
all over the world.

GARINISH ISLAND
Glengariff, Co. Cork
Tel.: (27) 63040
This island bathed by the warm
currents of the Gulf Stream in
Bantry Bay, at Ireland's most
southwesterly point, is an exotic
paradise set against the wild
Irish landscape.

JOHN F. KENNEDY ARBORETUM
New Ross, Co. Wexford
Tel.: (51) 388171
The Kennedy family's origins
in this region are the reason
behind the name of this
arboretum, which contains
an impressive variety of trees
and rare plants.

JOHNSTOWN CASTLE
Johnstown, Co. Wexford
Tel.: (53) 42888 *(p. 82)*
The Gothic Revival castle,
reflected in the waters of one of
the lakes in the gardens, makes
a magnificent setting for
the colors of its collection of
rhododendrons and camellias.

MOUNT STEWART
Newtownards, Co. Down
Northern Ireland
Tel.: (1247) 788387
One of the most impressive
gardens in Ireland, laid out
around the eighteenth-century
Mount Stewart House (also open
to the public), which contains a
spectacular collection of
furniture and works of art.

MOUNT USHER GARDENS
Ashford, Co. Wicklow
Tel.: (404) 40116
A perfect example of a romantic
garden, with a very fine
collection of rhododendrons. Tea
room and shop also available.

MUCKROSS HOUSE
Killarney, Co. Kerry
Tel.: (64) 31440
Beautiful gardens surrounding a
Victorian residence feature
massed rhododendrons, Scotch
pines, other exotic trees and
shrubs, and an arboretum.

NATIONAL BOTANIC GARDENS
Glasnevin, Dublin 9
Tel.: (1) 837 4388
Spectacular nineteenth-century glasshouses, recently restored, are one of the highlights of this outstanding botanical garden.

PALM HOUSE
Botanic Gardens
Stanmillis Road, Belfast
Tel.: (1232) 324902
These breathtaking glasshouses, a remarkable example of Victorian architecture, are the work of Richard Turner, who also designed the celebrated Palm House at London's Kew Gardens.

POWERSCOURT GARDENS
Enniskerry, Co. Wicklow
Tel.: (1286) 7676 *(p.78)*
The magnificent classical gardens at Powerscourt, close to Dublin, are famous throughout the world. Terraces with mosaics of black and white pebbles lead down to the lake. The Powerscourt cascade, in a romantic setting five kilometers away, should not be missed.

WHISKEY AND GUINNESS

Whiskey and Guinness, invented in a small Dublin brewery, are an essential part of Irish

culture. The following are some of the many places where they may be tasted.

MIDDLETON
Middleton, Co. Cork
Tel.: (21) 631821
This distillery, the most modern in the world, produces the greatest Irish whiskeys, including Jameson, Power, Paddy, and Tullamore Dew. The old distillery buildings have been converted into a visitor centre housing a museum, good restaurants, and shops as well as tasting rooms.

OLD BUSHMILLS DISTILLERY
Bushmills, Co. Antrim
Northern Ireland
Tel.: (1265) 731521
Bushmills is the world's oldest licensed brewery. In its picturesque setting near the Giant's Causeway, it produces the only single malt Irish whiskey.

THE IRISH WHISKEY CORNER
Bow Street, Dublin 8
Tel.: (1) 872 5566
Housed in the former Jameson brewery buildings, this small museum traces the long history of whiskey with the help of numerous objects and photographs, tastings, and a shop.

GOLF

Ireland offers 350 of the most famous and formidable golf course in the world, set in superb scenery. *The Golfer's Guide to Ireland* is available from the Tourist Board. *Golfing Ireland* (8 Parnell Square, Dublin, tel.: (1) 872 2611) undertakes to make reservations and draw up personalized itineraries.

GUINNESS HOPSTORE
James's Gate Street, Dublin 8
Tel.: (1) 408 4800
Set in a nineteenth-century warehouse in the heart of old Dublin, the Hopstore presents the history of the Guinness brewery, and the secrets of the brewing of the world's most famous stout.

BEWLEY'S ORIENTAL CAFE
78 Grafton Street, Dublin
Tel.: (1) 677 6761
Bewley's is a Dublin institution, with a chain of 24 delightful establishments—cafes, shops, or both—across Ireland. Here one can try the wonderful Irish

coffee: a mixture of coffee, whiskey, and cream.

BRAZEN HEAD
20 Lower Bridge Street, Dublin 2
Tel.: (1) 677 9549
This pub, a veritable historic monument, claims to be the oldest in Dublin. The atmosphere is friendly and crowded, and the decorations feature elaborate woodwork and old photographs.

DOHENY AND NESBITT
5 Lower Baggot Street, Dublin
Tel.: (1) 676 2945
A traditional pub which still retains its nineteenth-century alcoves for quiet conversations.

LONG HALL
South Great
51 George's Street, Dublin 2
Tel.: (1) 475 1590
The Victorian decor of this pub, with its polychrome ceiling moldings and crystal chandeliers, merits a special visit; the atmosphere of elegant sophistication is typical of old Irish pubs.

CROWN LIQUOR SALOON
46 Great Victoria Street, Belfast
Northern Ireland
Tel.: (1232) 325368
This magnificent Victorian bar

is a historic monument administered by the National Trust, which oversaw the restoration of its stucco, stained glass, marble, and mosaic decorations.

HARGADON BAR
4–5 O'Connell Street, Sligo
Tel.: (71) 70933
A Sligo institution, this pub has survived the passing decades unchanged, complete with traditional woodstove, numerous snugs, all ancient and different, and a wooden counter.

Other interesting traditional pubs include:

MARBLE CITY BAR
66 High Street, Kilkenny
Tel.: (56) 62091
MULLIGAN'S
8 Poolbeg Street, Dublin
Tel.: (1) 677 5582
NEARY'S
1 Chatham Street, Dublin
Tel.: (1) 677 8596
RYAN'S
28 Parkgate Street, Dublin
Tel.: (1) 677 6097

This pub is famous for its beautiful Victorian-style interior (carved wood, stained glass, and several snugs), as well as its convivial atmosphere.

This work is adapted from certain
elements of a book created by Stewart,
Tabori & Chang, New York, titled *In the
Houses of Ireland*, published in France
under the title *L'art de vivre en Irelande*.

All photographs are by Walter Pfeiffer.
Text adapted from Odile Laversanne's
translation of Marianne Héron's texts.
Translation from the French by
Barbara Mellor.

Editorial Director: Ghislaine
Bavoillot
Artistic Director:
Marc Walter

ISBN: 2-08013-585-6
Numéro d'édition: 1332
Dépôt légal: May 1997
Printed in Italy

Library of Congress Catalog
Card Number: 97-060628

Typesetting by
Octavo Editions, Paris
Color separation by
Colourscan, France
Printed by Canale, Turin

The map of the Irish counties
on this page is reproduced by
kind permission of the Irish
Tourist Board. The shaded
area indicates the six counties
of Northern Ireland.

Flammarion
26 rue Racine
75006 Paris

200 Park Avenue South
Suite 1406
New York, NY 10003

DONEGAL
DERRY
ANTRIM
TYRONE
FERMANAGH
MONAGHAN
ARMAGH
DOWN
Belfast
SLIGO
LEITRIM
CAVAN
MAYO
ROSCOMMON
LONGFORD
LOUTH
MEATH
WESTMEATH
GALWAY
OFFALY
KILDARE
DUBLIN
LAOIS
WICKLOW
CLARE
CARLOW
LIMERICK
TIPPERARY
KILKENNY
WEXFORD
KERRY
CORK
WATERFORD